RIVER
ADVENTURES

THAMES

W

FRANKLIN WATTS
LONDON•SYDNEY

First published 2012 by Franklin Watts
338 Euston Road
London NW1 3BH

Franklin Watts Australia
Level 17/207 Kent Street
Sydney, NSW 2000

Design, editing and picture research by Paul Manning
Maps by Stefan Chabluk
Proofread and indexed by Alice Harman

Produced for Franklin Watts by
White-Thomson Publishing Ltd

www.wtpub.co.uk
+44 (0) 845 362 8240

A CIP catalogue record for this book is available from
the British Library.

ISBN 978 1 4451 1036 3

Dewey classification: 914.2'2

Key to images

Top cover image: The Thames Barrier at Woolwich
Main cover image: Tower Bridge, with HMS *Belfast*
in the foreground.
Previous page: A mother swan and cygnets
on the Thames.
This page: A panorama of the Thames
at Westminster.

Note to Teachers and Parents

Every effort has been made to ensure that the websites
listed on page 32 are suitable for children, that they
are of the highest educational vaue and that they
contain no inappropriate or offensive material. However,
because of the nature of the internet, it is impossible
to guarantee that the content of these sites will not be
altered. We strongly recommend that internet access is
supervised by a responsible adult.

Printed in China

Franklin Watts is a division of Hachette
Children's Books,
an Hachette UK company
www.hachette.co.uk

Picture Credits

CONTENTS

A Thames Journey

The River Thames is famous for its history, scenery and wildlife. It follows a winding course through southern England, flowing from the Cotswold hills east towards London and beyond. You will follow its 352-km (218-mile) journey from source to sea.

▼ The Thames is the longest river entirely in England, and the second longest in the UK. Before reaching London, it passes through several other towns, including Oxford, Reading and Windsor.

England's river

The Thames has shaped England's landscape since prehistoric times. In the first century CE, Roman London grew up on its banks. In the 18th and 19th centuries, ships travelled the river carrying raw materials from all over the British Empire. Many famous events took place on or near the Thames, and your journey will take you past many of England's best-known landmarks.

A cleaner river

Sixty years ago, the Thames was so badly polluted that scientists thought it would never recover. In the 1960s, a big clean-up began, and fish once more began to appear in it. Now, it is one of the world's least polluted urban rivers.

Where is the source?

The Thames starts as a tiny spring bubbling out of the ground at Thames Head, near the village of Kemble in Gloucestershire. Or does it? Some say it should really be measured from a place called Severn Springs, near Andoversford, 18 km (11 miles) further north. Severn Springs is the source of the River Churn, which joins the Thames at Cricklade.

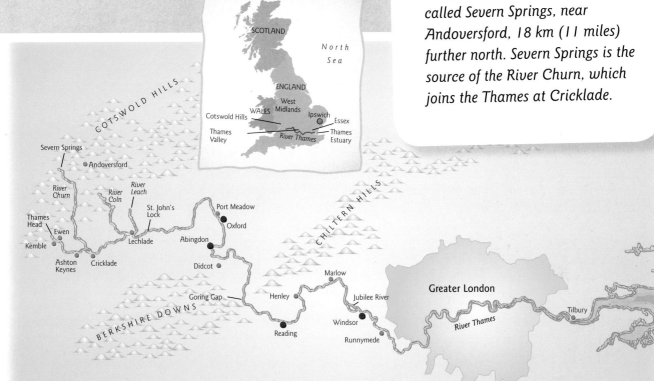

SCOTLAND

North Sea

ENGLAND

West Midlands

WALES

Cotswold Hills

Ipswich

Essex

Thames Valley

River Thames

Thames Estuary

COTSWOLD HILLS

Severn Springs

Andoversford

River Churn

River Coln

River Leach

St. John's Lock

Port Meadow

Oxford

Thames Head

Ewen

Kemble

Lechlade

Abingdon

Ashton Keynes

Cricklade

Didcot

CHILTERN HILLS

Marlow

Greater London

Goring Gap

Henley

Jubilee River

Tilbury

BERKSHIRE DOWNS

Windsor

River Thames

Reading

Runnymede

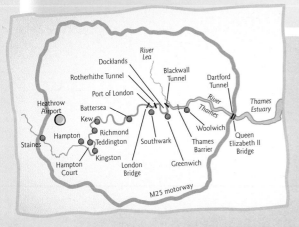

River Lea

Docklands

Blackwall Tunnel

Dartford Tunnel

Rotherhithe Tunnel

Port of London

River Thames

Thames Estuary

Heathrow Airport

Battersea

Kew

Woolwich

Hampton

Richmond

Teddington

Southwark

Thames Barrier

Queen Elizabeth II Bridge

Staines

Kingston

Greenwich

Hampton Court

London Bridge

M25 motorway

▶ Otters once disappeared from the Thames, but are slowly returning as the river becomes cleaner.

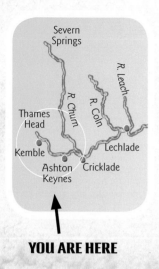

YOU ARE HERE

The Cotswolds

For the first part of its journey, the Thames is little more than a stream flowing through the Cotswold countryside. The river here is too shallow for boats, so you have to follow the route on foot.

Soon after leaving Kemble, you pass the pretty Cotswold village of Ashton Keynes. Many of the cottages here are reached by their own tiny stone bridge across the river. The water is crystal clear, and you can see shoals of tiny fish darting among the weeds.

▼ *This shady stretch of the river is a perfect place to fish for minnows.*

Thames tributaries

On its journey, the Thames is joined by many smaller streams called tributaries which add to its flow. Near Cricklade, it is joined by the Churn. A little further on at Lechlade, the Leach and Coln flow into it too, and the water becomes deep enough for boats. The Thames has 50 tributaries in all, not including canals.

▲ *In earlier times, Lechlade, just beyond this lock, was the highest point on the river which could be reached by barge.*

In the Middle Ages, barges travelled from Lechlade, carrying goods to market in London. There were also mills along the river, where water power was used to grind corn.

▶ *These rare wild flowers are called snake's head fritillaries. They are only found in flood meadows beside the Thames.*

7

The Isis

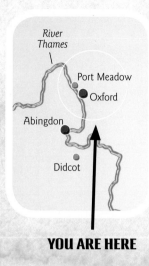

At Oxford, the Thames is called the Isis, from its Latin name 'Tame-isis'. Oxford gets its name from the words 'oxen ford' – the place where oxen cross ('ford') the river.

Port Meadow

As you approach the city, a huge field known as Port Meadow opens out on your left. In the winter, the meadow is often covered in water which freezes to form a natural ice-rink. Low-lying fields like this are very important for absorbing floodwater from the river, and as a wildlife habitat. Many meadows are disappearing as land is used for arable farming or for housing.

▼ Folly Bridge, south of the city, is Oxford's oldest river crossing. Cattle forded the Thames here in ancient times.

◄ The river at Oxford is widely used for sport, leisure and recreation.

A university town

Closer to the city centre, you see a cluster of spires, domes and old buildings. Many have fine lawns and gardens stretching down to the river. These are the colleges of Oxford University.

Oxford has been a university town since the 13th century, when religious scholars founded the first colleges. During term-time, the streets are crowded with students on bicycles. Huge numbers of tourists come to Oxford to visit the university and its buildings.

Sport on the river

Rowing has been popular in Oxford since the eighteenth century, when college crews called 'eights' first started to hold races on the river. Today the big event is the University Boat Race, held between Putney and Mortlake in London each year, when Oxford take on their arch-rivals, Cambridge.

► Riverside walks and fine buildings like the Radcliffe Camera attract many visitors to Oxford.

The Thames Valley

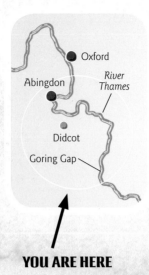

YOU ARE HERE

Beyond Oxford, the Thames winds through gently rolling countryside. The land here is very fertile and has supported human life for thousands of years.

▼ Abingdon, south of Oxford, is one of Britain's oldest towns. There has been a settlement here for at least 6,000 years.

Natural resources

In prehistoric times, the Thames Valley was a good place to live. People grew crops and grazed their cattle by the river. As well as fresh water, the Thames provided fish to eat and a wide range of natural resources, such as reeds, rushes and timber for building. The river bed was also full of flint, which was useful for making sharp tools like axes.

◀ At the Goring Gap, the Thames heads south between the Chiltern Hills and the Berkshire Downs.

The Goring Gap

At Goring, near Reading, the sides of the valley become steeper. The landscape here has been dramatically shaped by the river.

Originally, the Thames followed a northeasterly route, rising in the West Midlands and flowing through Hertfordshire and Essex into the North Sea near Ipswich. After the last Ice Age, torrents of water from melting glaciers forced the river to change course. Instead of flowing northeast, the Thames carved its way south, creating the gorge called the Goring Gap.

Soil erosion

As a river flows, the force of its moving water washes away loose soil and rock. In this way, the river cuts its own channel in the ground. The process of wearing away rocks is called erosion. With a slow-moving river like the Thames, erosion can take place gradually over thousands of years.

▶ Eel, salmon and trout have been caught in the Thames since ancient times. These anglers have landed a pike.

11

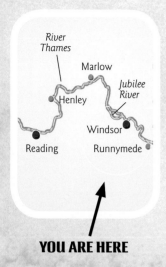

River Thames

Marlow

Henley

Jubilee River

Windsor

Reading

Runnymede

YOU ARE HERE

A Royal River

After Reading, the Thames heads north to Henley, before turning east and south again towards Marlow. Further downriver, you catch your first sight of Windsor Castle.

▼ The river is a natural barrier protecting the castle at Windsor.

A defensive site

Windsor Castle began as a wooden fort built at the time of the Norman Conquest. William the Conqueror chose the site because it overlooked the river and was easy to defend. As the castle grew, the town of Windsor grew up around it. Today, the castle is one of the main homes of the British royal family, and a popular tourist site.

The Jubilee River

Windsor Castle is well protected on its high mound, but the land around it has often been affected by floods. In 1947, the river rose to around 2 m (6 ft) higher than usual. Large areas were flooded, and many people were trapped in their homes. In 2001, a special channel called the Jubilee River was created to protect the region from flooding.

Runnymede

Shortly after Windsor, you pass the water meadow of Runnymede. On the north bank is a small island where, in 1215, King John is believed to have signed Magna Carta. This 'great charter' was the first successful attempt to limit the power of the king and protect the rights of English people. The name 'runnymede' means 'a meeting place in the meadow'.

'Swan Upping'

Swan counting, or 'upping', goes back to the time when all swans belonged to the king or queen, and numbers were regularly checked. Today, swans can be seen all along the Thames, but many are injured by fishing lines and hooks, or affected by pollution in the water.

▶ *Boatmen carry out the annual task of counting swans on the Thames near Windsor. Each swan is checked for disease and injury before being placed back in the water.*

Greater London

M25 Ringroad

River Thames

Heathrow Airport

Staines

YOU ARE HERE

As you approach London, the landscape changes. Jets fly overhead, bound for Heathrow Airport, and the river passes under the M25, London's busy motorway ringroad.

The 'commuter belt'

On this part of your journey, you pass through some of the most densely populated parts of the UK. More than 8 million people live in Greater London, and many businesses are located here because of its transport and communications links. This is also the city's 'commuter belt', where people live and travel to work in central London. All these people need water.

▼ *These lakes and reservoirs on the outskirts of London are for storing water from the Thames.*

◀ At this treatment works, wastewater from homes and factories is decontaminated before being fed back into the river.

Who needs water?

Roughly 79 per cent of London's water is used in people's homes. The rest is used by industries, including breweries and paper-makers. Some of the biggest users are power stations like the one at Didcot in Berkshire, where Thames water is used to cool the giant electricity turbines.

Lakes and reservoirs

At Staines, the Thames heads south, criss-crossing under roads and motorways and weaving among lakes and reservoirs.

As well as being a place for recreation and a transport route, the river is a vital source of water for London. Every day, millions of litres of water from the Thames are diverted to lakes and reservoirs. Water is then pumped to treatment works, to be cleaned and filtered before being piped to people's homes.

▶ At a Thames Water laboratory, a scientist examines a water sample to make sure it is clean and safe to drink.

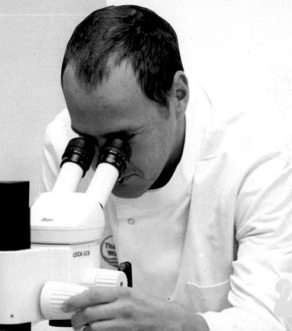

The Tidal Thames

River Thames

Kew

Richmond

Hampton

Teddington

Hampton Court

Kingston

YOU ARE HERE

At Teddington Lock, you reach an important stage in your journey. Here, fresh water meets salt water carried in from the sea. From now on, the Thames is a tidal river.

▼ Teddington Weir marks the start of the tidal section of the Thames, known as the Tideway.

The tide effect

Although the sea is nearly 104 km (65 miles) away, the tide has a big effect on the river. Instead of flowing steadily out towards the sea, the fresh water heading downstream is pushed back by the incoming tide. Depending on the strength of the tide, the water that flows over Teddington Weir can take anything from three weeks to three months to reach the sea.

▶ Hampton Court was well connected to London by river. Over the palace gate, a clock still shows the time of high tide at London Bridge.

Parks and palaces

Between Hampton and Kew, the river is famous for its stately homes and royal parks and palaces. Many of these sites were chosen because of their riverside location.

Hampton Court was the favourite palace of Henry VIII. Kings, queens and important people often travelled this stretch of the river in royal barges. Travelling with the tide made the journey much quicker, so trips up and downriver were carefully timed.

Controlling the tide

At Richmond, a very low tide could mean that the river was little more than a shallow stream. Under this bridge, a barrage has been built with gates which can be raised and lowered. This protects boats moored upstream from running aground when the tide goes out.

◀ The barrage at Richmond helps to control the effect of the tide.

The Working River

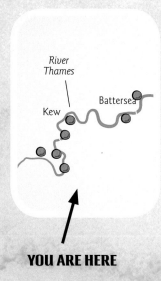

River
Thames

Kew

Battersea

YOU ARE HERE

After the green spaces of Richmond and Kew, you are now in urban West London. Here, the river is lined with offices, flats, warehouses and industrial buildings.

A transport route

▼ Battersea Power Station once produced electricity for the whole of London, but has been disused since 1982. Coal was brought by river every day and unloaded by cranes which still stand on the waterfront.

In the past, the river was a vital transport route. Many industries were based along its banks, and ships and barges carried supplies of coal and other raw materials which were unloaded at wharves on the waterfront.

◀ Barges towed by tugboats were once a common sight on the river. Today, most heavy goods are carried by road or rail.

As London grew, road and rail transport gradually took over from boats, and use of the river declined. Today, a few working boats can be seen, but most of the traffic on the river is made up of tourist or pleasure boats.

Bridges and tunnels

Until the 18th century, London Bridge was the only place in London where the river could be crossed. Today, there are 33 bridges across the Thames between Hampton and Southwark. Pedestrian and rail tunnels have also been built underneath the Thames, and there are road tunnels at Blackwall, Rotherhithe and Dartford.

Commuting by river

Riverbus is a good way to travel this stretch of the Thames. There are no traffic jams, and you can enjoy some of the best views of London from the river. More than 2,000 commuters a day now travel to work on the Thames. Catching a riverbus is as easy as catching a bus or underground train.

Westminster

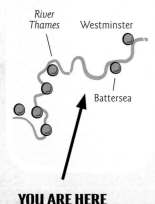

River Thames Westminster

Battersea

YOU ARE HERE

At Westminster, your boat ride takes you past some of London's most historic buildings. Since 1066, 38 English kings and queens have been crowned in Westminster Abbey, and laws have been debated in the Houses of Parliament since the 13th century.

▼ *The Houses of Parliament overlook the Thames at Westminster.*

▶ The Millennium Footbridge connects the South Bank with St Paul's Cathedral. It is the newest bridge over the Thames.

The Embankment

The Thames here flows between high stone walls called embankments. These were built in Victorian times to protect the city from flooding. Before this, the river was flanked on either side by muddy land. Much of London's sewage ended up here, and many Londoners died from diseases caused by drinking water from the river.

The London Eye

On the north bank, the Victoria Embankment carries a steady stream of traffic east and west through the city. On the other side of the river is the giant ferris wheel known as the London Eye. From the top of this, you have a far-reaching view of the Thames as it flows through London.

▶ London's embankments and sewers were built by Joseph Bazalgette (1819–91). His memorial stands on the Victoria Embankment.

The 'Great Stink'

During a heatwave in 1858, the smell of sewage in the Thames became so bad that Parliament had to be suspended. Afterwards, the government decided to build a huge new system of tunnels to get rid of the city's waste. The new sewers stopped drinking water from being contaminated by sewage. This saved the lives of thousands of Londoners.

FLVM'N' VINC'LA P°SV'T

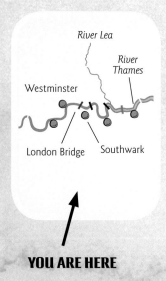

YOU ARE HERE

▼ *The earliest crossing at London Bridge was built of wood. The present stone bridge dates from 1973. It leads directly to the City of London financial district.*

The Port of London

A river crossing has existed on the site of London Bridge since Roman times. It was here that London began, as a tiny settlement on the banks of the Thames.

An ancient crossing

The first bridge over the Thames was built by the Romans in around 50 CE. The Romans chose the site carefully: it was the furthest point inland where seagoing ships could anchor in the tidal waters of the Thames. On the river banks, a port was built where goods could be unloaded, and the Roman town of Londinium grew up around it.

River trade

The river has brought wealth to London ever since. In the 18th and 19th centuries, London was the busiest port in the world. There were so many vessels on the Thames, it was said that you could cross the river by stepping from one ship to the next!

The growth of the docks

The original Port of London was based between London Bridge and Wapping. As trade increased, shipping companies built their own docks further downstream. The last to be built was King George V dock, in 1921.

▲ Tower Bridge at the entrance to the old Port of London has sections of road called bascules. These can be raised to let tall ships through.

The Thames Tunnel

The Thames Tunnel at Rotherhithe was the world's first underwater tunnel. It was built by the engineer Isambard Kingdom Brunel and his father Mark Isambard Brunel between 1825 and 1843. Digging under the riverbed was highly dangerous, and there were often floods when the roof collapsed, and mud and water poured in.

Docklands

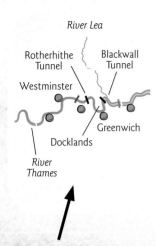

River Lea
Rotherhithe Tunnel
Blackwall Tunnel
Westminster
Greenwich
Docklands
River Thames

YOU ARE HERE

As you head east from Tower Bridge, you can see a cluster of high-rise blocks ahead of you. These are the giant towers of London's Docklands.

▼ *The business and financial district at Canary Wharf is the heart of modern Docklands. Around 90,000 people work here.*

The end of the docks

Over the last 30 years this area has changed a lot. In the 1960s, the London docks began to close down one by one, as trade shifted to bigger ports near the sea. Within a few years the docks had become a derelict wasteland.

In the 1980s, a huge building project transformed the old warehouses and wharves into new riverside communities. Smart new flats and offices were built around the dock basins. By 1998, more than 24,000 new homes had been built, and 2,700 new businesses had moved into the area.

Policing the Thames

A naval town

At Greenwich, you break your journey to visit the National Maritime Museum and Royal Observatory. On display are the famous Harrison Clocks that first allowed sailors to plot their position accurately on long sea voyages. Greenwich is also the home of the *Cutty Sark*, a great tall-masted sailing ship that once raced to bring back cargoes of tea from China.

Since 1800, crime-fighting on the river has been the job of the Thames River Police. In the past, smuggling was common, and cargo ships on the Thames were often a target for river pirates. Today, police launches are more likely to be on the lookout for drug-runners and people-traffickers.

▶ *Tourist boats and riverbuses bring visitors to the old Royal Naval College at Greenwich.*

The Thames Barrier

Around the site of the O2 Arena at Greenwich, the river turns a tight loop. Ahead of you now are the giant piers of the Thames Barrier.

YOU ARE HERE

Queen Elizabeth II Road Bridge

Thames Barrier

Woolwich

Greenwich

M25 Ringroad

Dartford Tunnel

▼ *East of London, the landscape is flat and low-lying. Many industries are based here. This part of the river was once badly polluted by chemicals and other waste.*

The Thames Barrier

The Thames Barrier has been in place since 1984. It is London's main defence against flooding. Between the piers are huge curved gates below the water. Normally the gates are lowered to allow ships to pass through. When the flood risk is high, the gates are raised to hold back the tide.

◀ The Thames Barrier spans a 520-m (1,706-ft) wide section of the Thames at Woolwich.

What is a surge tide?

When storms at sea coincide with high tides, a surge tide can sweep upriver, causing flooding and widespread destruction. London is at risk because much of the land on which it is built is low-lying. Experts say the city is sinking at a rate of 30 cm (12 in) every 100 years.

The Thames Barrier is only part of London's flood defences. There are 36 other, smaller barriers, and more than 185 km (115 miles) of defence walls along the riverbanks. On average, the Thames Barrier closes three times a year to protect London from surge tides from the sea. Luckily, no high storm tides are forecast today, so you can continue safely on your way.

▶ The Queen Elizabeth II road bridge crosses the river at Dartford. The height of the bridge allows cruise ships to pass under it on their way to the Port of London.

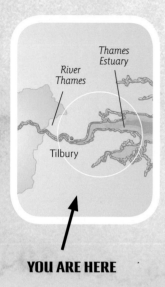

River Thames

Thames Estuary

Tilbury

YOU ARE HERE

The Thames Estuary

As the Thames flows out towards the sea, it opens out into a broad expanse of mudflats and salt marshes. Your river journey is nearly over.

A shipping route

This part of the Thames is a busy route for oil tankers, container ships, bulk carriers and ferries. The river is wide and slow-moving at this point. Parts of it are flanked by wide banks called levées which protect the land on either side from flooding.

▼ Egypt Bay on the Thames Estuary was once a favourite spot for smugglers bringing stolen goods ashore.

Tilbury

In ancient times, Tilbury was important in defending the river from enemy ships and preventing attacks on London. Today, Tilbury Docks is one of the busiest ports in the UK, handling passenger ships and container vessels from all over the world.

The future

As London continues to grow, the future of the Thames Estuary is uncertain. With the completion of the high-speed Channel Tunnel Rail Link, the region is set to become a centre for new jobs and housing. London's fourth airport may be located here too.

New development will certainly bring wealth, but many are concerned about the impact on wildlife, especially the many wading birds that live in the area.

▲ A container ship heads up the estuary towards Tilbury Docks.

Thames barges

Thames barges were perfect for sailing the shallow waters of the Thames Estuary, and restored barges still sail the river today. Built of wood with huge sails, the barges were originally used to transport bricks, sand, coal and grain. Over time, they were gradually replaced by steam-powered vessels.

Glossary

arable farming growing crops in a field

barrage a barrier to halt or reduce the flow of a river

cholera a deadly disease spread by dirty water

commuter a person who travels to work by car, bus or train

container ship a ship that transports goods in steel crates

course the route followed by a river

decline to reduce or become less

decontaminate to clean or remove impurities from something

derelict abandoned and run-down

embankment a high wall used to contain the flow of a river

erosion the gradual wearing away of soil or rock

fertile good for growing

ford a place where a river is shallow and can be crossed

gorge a deep river valley with steep rocky sides

Ice Age a time long ago when the temperature dropped and the Earth was covered with ice

lock a device for lifting or lowering boats from one level of water to another

minnow a tiny fish that lives in shallow water

Norman Conquest the time from 1066 onwards when Britain was conquered by the Normans

pedestrian a person who travels on foot

polluted made dirty, e.g. by sewage

reservoir a lake used to store water

salt marsh an area of muddy land in a coastal area

scholar a person who spends their time studying

settlement a place where people live permanently

source the beginning of a river, usually a lake or spring

suspended cancelled or abandoned

tideway the part of a river that is affected by tides

tributary a stream or river that flows into another, bigger one

turbine a wheel that is turned by water to produce electricity

urban belonging to a town or city

wastewater water that has been washed down a drain

water meadow a field that is partly flooded at certain times of year

weir a type of dam used to control the flow of a river

wharf (*pl.* **wharves**) a place beside a river where goods are unloaded

Thames Quiz*

Find the answers in this book, or look them up online.

1 Match the captions to the pictures.

A The London Eye

B A pier of the Thames Barrier at Woolwich

C The statue of the Sphinx on the Victoria Embankment

D A deer in Windsor Great Park

E Punting on the river at Oxford

F The statue of 'Old Father Thames' at Lechlade Lock

2 These places can all be found along the Thames. Put them in the right order, starting with the ones nearest to the sea:

Windsor
Hampton Court
Tilbury Docks
Abingdon
Lechlade
Battersea

3 True or false?

'The Thames was once a tributary of the River Rhine that flows through Germany.'

4 This bronze head is on display in the British Museum. Do you know who it represents, and where it was found?

Websites and Further Reading

Websites

- www.primaryhomeworkhelp.co.uk/
  riverthames
  A detailed and well-illustrated virtual
  journey down the Thames.
- www.museumoflondon.org.uk/Explore-
  online/Pocket-histories/thames-in-
  prehistory
  Interesting information about the early
  history of the river.

- www.the-river-thames.co.uk
  A great source of facts and figures
  about the Thames.

Further Reading

Rivers (The Geography Detective Investigates series), Jen Green (Wayland, 2006)

River (Your Local Area series), Ruth Thomson (Wayland, 2010)

Index

Answers to Thames Quiz

1 1D, 2F, 3C, 4E, 5A, 6B. **2** Tilbury Docks, Battersea, Hampton Court, Windsor, Abingdon, Lechlade. **3** True. Before Britain was separated from continental Europe, the two rivers met in the area now covered by southern North Sea. **4** The bronze head is part of a statue of the Roman Emperor Hadrian. It was found buried in the mud below London Bridge in 1834.